THE MUSIC TREE
ACTIVITIES

PART I

by
Frances Clark
Louise Goss
Sam Holland
Steve Betts

Educational Consultants:

Steve Betts   Yat Yee Chong
Linda Christensen   Ted Cooper
Amy Glennon   Monica Hochstedler
Peter Jutras   Elvina Pearce
Mary Frances Reyburn Craig Sale

ISBN 0-87487-950-7

PREFACE

We are proud to present this latest revision of **THE MUSIC TREE,** the most carefully researched and laboratory-tested series for elementary piano students available. This edition combines the best of the old and the new—a natural, child-oriented sequence of learning experiences that has always been the hallmark of Frances Clark materials, combined with new music of unprecedented variety and appeal. Great pedagogy and great music—a winning combination!

THE MUSIC TREE consists of the eight books listed below, to be used in sequence. Each has a textbook and an activities book to be used together:

TEXTBOOKS	ACTIVITIES BOOKS
TIME TO BEGIN (the primer)	**TIME TO BEGIN ACTIVITIES**
MUSIC TREE 1 (formerly A)	**ACTIVITIES 1**
MUSIC TREE 2A (formerly B)	**ACTIVITIES 2A**
MUSIC TREE 2B (formerly C)	**ACTIVITIES 2B**

Used together, these companion volumes provide a comprehensive plan for musical growth at the piano and prepare for the intermediate materials that follow at Levels 3 and 4.

We are deeply indebted to the students and faculty of The New School for Music Study and the Southern Methodist University Preparatory Department, who have been the inspiration and proving ground for this new edition, and to our educational consultants who have reviewed and tested the materials at every step of their development.

These are among the last materials on which Frances Clark was able to work personally, and it is to her memory that the books are lovingly dedicated.

It is our hope that **THE MUSIC TREE** will provide for you the same success and delight in teaching that we have experienced, and that your students will share with ours the excitement of this new adventure in learning.

CONTENTS

Landmarks: F, C, and G

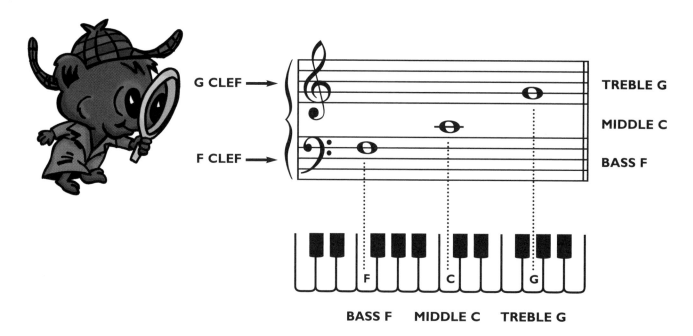

Circle each Landmark — then play and name it.
The first example is done to show you how.

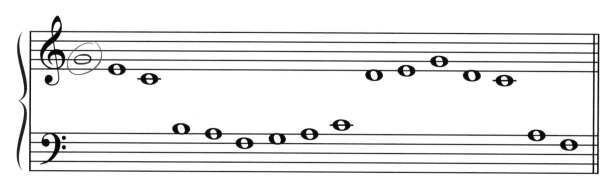

How many Treble Gs did you circle? _____ Bass Fs?_____ Middle Cs?_____

Fill in the landmark in each measure — then play and name it.
The first example is done to show you how.

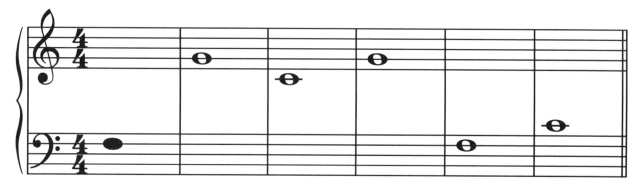

The Interval of a 2nd

2nds on the keyboard

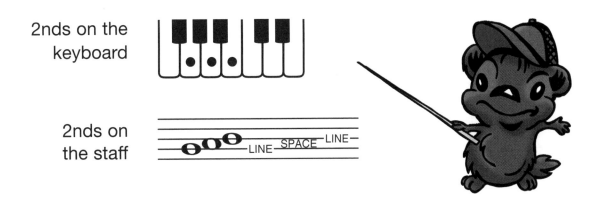

2nds on the staff

In this jumble, circle all the keyboards that have 2nds.

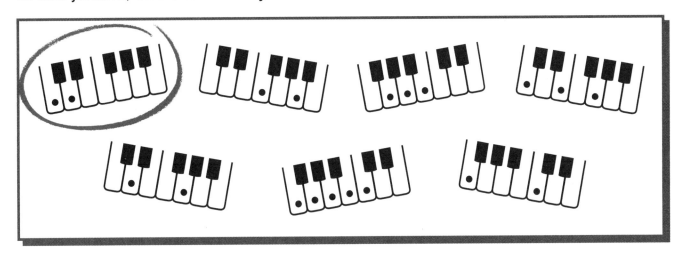

With RH fingers 234, play and name 2nds up from Landmarks:

    from Treble G

    from Middle C

    from Bass F

With LH fingers 234, play and name 2nds down from Landmarks:

    from Treble G

    from Middle C

    from Bass F

In this jumble, circle all the 2nds.

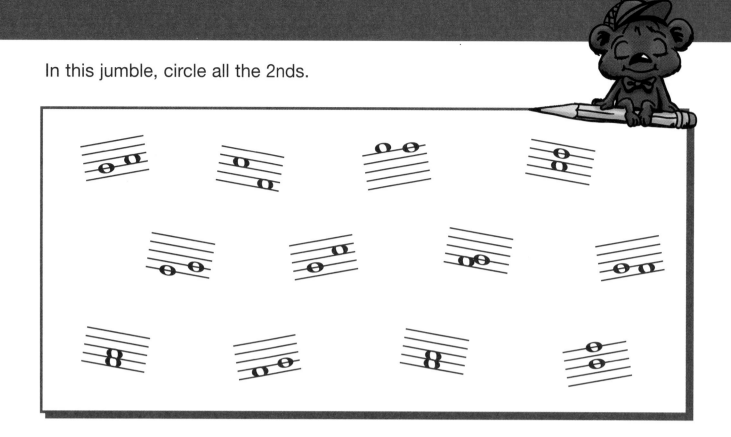

Mark all the 2nds.

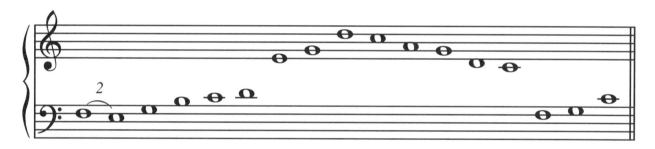

Write 2nds from Landmark to Landmark.

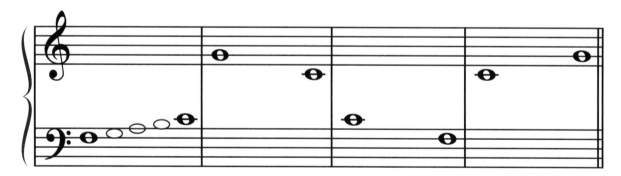

Rhythm

A quarter note gets 1 pulse	♩	—
A half note gets 2 pulses	♩	——
A dotted half note gets 3 pulses	♩.	———
A whole note gets 4 pulses	𝅝	————

Time Signature **4/4** = **4** pulses in each measure
♩ gets 1 pulse

1. Swing and say the rhyme with a strong rhythmic pulse, one swing for each pulse.

Sing a Song of Sixpence

Sing   a   song   of   six - pence,   Pock - et   full   of   rye,

Four   and   twen - ty   black - birds,   Baked   in   a   pie!

2. Say the rhyme again, drawing lines under the words, one line for each pulse.

 ♩   ♩ _   ♩. _ _   𝅝 _ _ _

3. Then walk the rhythm as you say the rhyme, taking one step for each pulse.

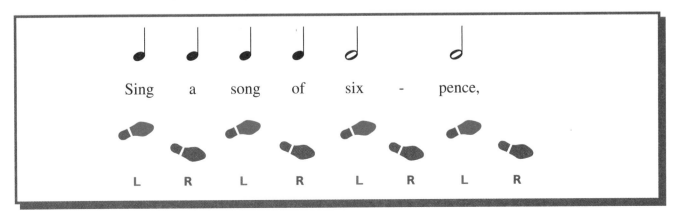

Sing   a   song   of   six   -   pence,

L   R   L   R   L   R   L   R

7

Sight-Playing

Sight-playing is playing a piece **at first sight** without any practice.

1. Circle the clef. Then prepare your hand/s and fingers on the correct keys.

2. Set a **slow** tempo, counting two measures out loud in a strong rhythmic pulse.

3. Play and count with a full tone, **no stopping** from beginning to end.

Except for No. 5, play each piece in the clef in which it is written, then an octave higher or lower with the other hand.

1.

2.

3.

4.

5.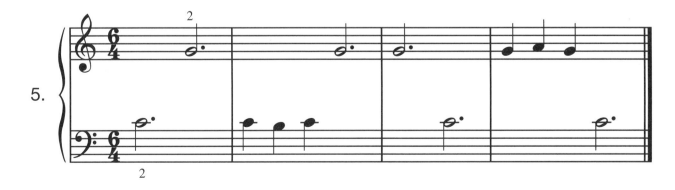

*See explanation of stems in music.

Matching

Mark an X through the interval in each box that does not match.

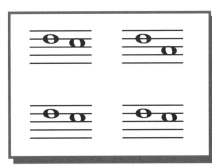

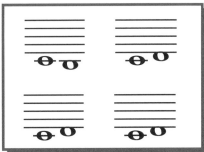

Draw a line to connect each sign with its name.

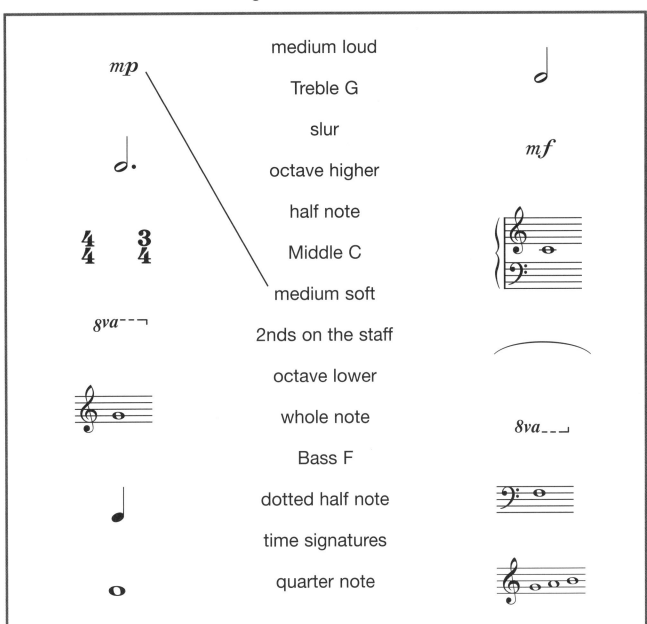

medium loud

Treble G

slur

octave higher

half note

Middle C

medium soft

2nds on the staff

octave lower

whole note

Bass F

dotted half note

time signatures

quarter note

Beginning a 2nd Above Landmarks

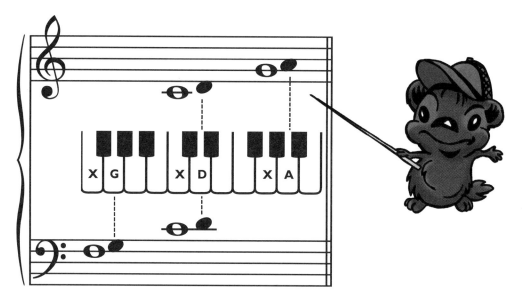

Write the name of the key a 2nd **above** each checked key.

Keyboard Dictation

Play each group of intervals and write the name of the last note.

    The letter shows the starting key.
    The number shows the interval.
    The slanting lines show which direction to play.

The first one is done to show you how.

RH, begin with finger 2:

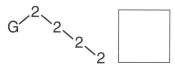

LH, begin with finger 2:

Your answers should spell a word!

Spot-Placing

Spot-placing is finding a note from the nearest Landmark.

For example, to spot-place this note:

put an X on the nearest Landmark

and name the note, "Treble G, up a 2nd, A."

Each of these notes is a 2nd above a Landmark. To find each note:
- Put an X on the Landmark line.
- Spot-place the note.
- Write its name in the box.
- Then play and name the note.

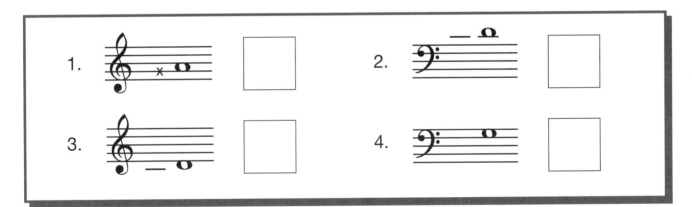

2nds on the Staff

Draw the note a 2nd **above** each of these notes.

Draw the note a 2nd **below** each of these notes.

Add the time signature to each of these rhythms.

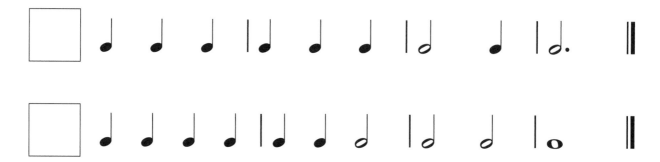

Now point and count to check your work.

1. Swing and say the rhyme with a strong rhythmic pulse —
   one swing for each pulse.

Dessert Time

2. Say the rhyme again, drawing lines under the words —
   one line for each pulse.

3. Then walk the rhythm as you say the rhyme, taking one step for each pulse.

Add measure bars and an ending bar to each of these rhythms.

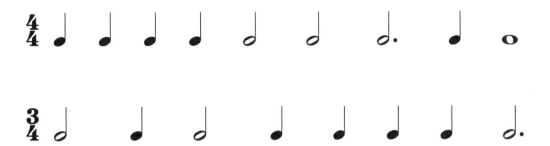

Now point and count to check your work.

Rhythm Detective

Find and circle the measures that have too many pulses.

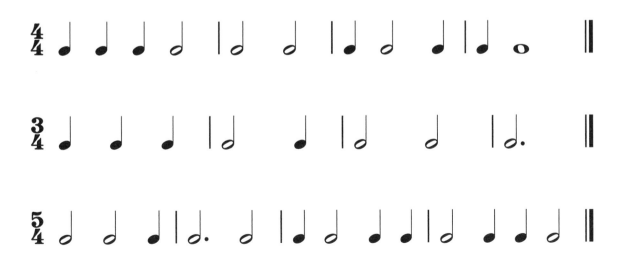

Sight-Playing

Sight-playing is playing a piece **at first sight** without any practice.

1. Circle the clef. Then prepare your hand/s and fingers on the correct keys.

2. Set a **slow** tempo, counting two measures out loud in a strong rhythmic pulse.

3. Play and count with a full tone, **no stopping** from beginning to end.

Except for No. 5, play each piece in the clef in which it is written, then an octave higher or lower with the other hand.

Which One?

Circle the correct music for each group of letter names.
The first one is done to show you how.

Example:

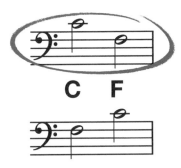

C   F

C C D

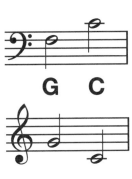

G   C

F G F

F   F

G G A

Beginning a 2nd Below Landmarks

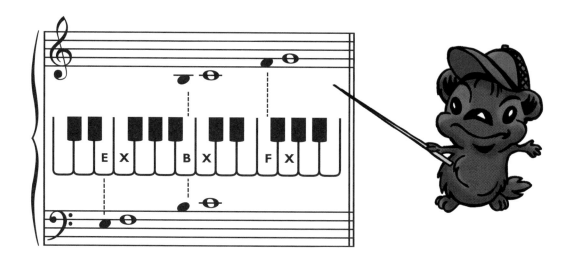

Write the name of the key a 2nd **below** each checked key.

Keyboard Dictation

Play each group of intervals and write the name of the last note.

RH, begin with finger 2:

LH, begin with finger 2:

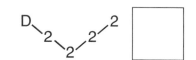

For correlated Discoveries, Repertoire and Technic, see MUSIC TREE 1, pages 15-20.

Spot-Placing

To find each note:

- Put an X on the Landmark line.
- Spot-place the note and write its name in the box.
- Then play and name the note.

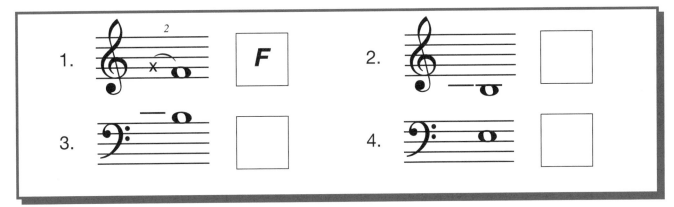

Each of these notes is a 2nd **above** or **below** a Landmark.

To find each note:

- Put an X on the Landmark line.
- On the blank line under each note, write its name.

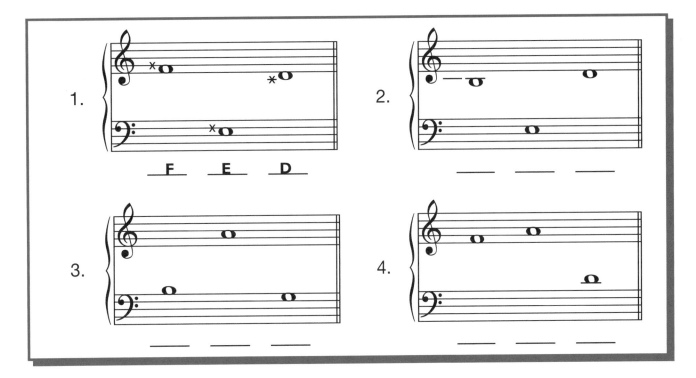

Your answers should spell a word.

Rhythm

1. Swing and say the rhyme with a strong rhythmic pulse —
   one swing for each pulse.

Rubber Boots

We   are   wear - ing   rub - ber   boots,   on   this   rain - y   day.

Keep - ing   warm   and   dry   a -   long   the   mud - dy   way.

2. Say the rhyme again, drawing lines under the words —
   one line for each pulse

3. Then walk the rhythm as you say the rhyme,
   taking one step for each pulse.

Add the time signature to each of these rhythms.

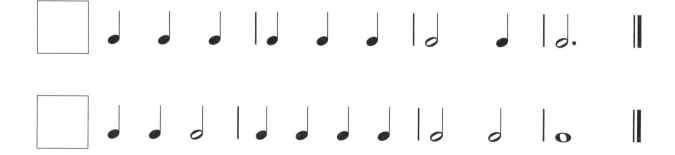

18

Add measure bars and an ending bar to each of these rhythms.

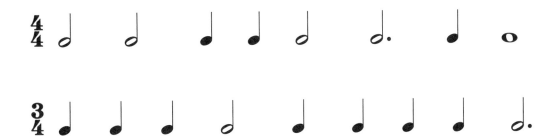

In each of these rhythms, set a strong rhythmic pulse:

1. Point and count — point to each note as you count aloud.
2. Tap and count — tap lightly with your fingertips on the keyboard cover or a table — one tap for each **note**.

Notes **above** the line are for RH. Notes **below** the line are for LH.

Sight-Playing

1. Circle the clef. Then prepare your hand/s and fingers on the correct keys.

2. Set a **slow** tempo, counting two measures out loud in a strong rhythmic pulse.

3. Play and count with a full tone, **no stopping** from beginning to end.

Except for No. 5, play each piece in the clef in which it is written, then an octave higher or lower with the other hand.

1.

2.

3.

4.

5.

Crossword Puzzle

Draw a line to connect each sign with its name.

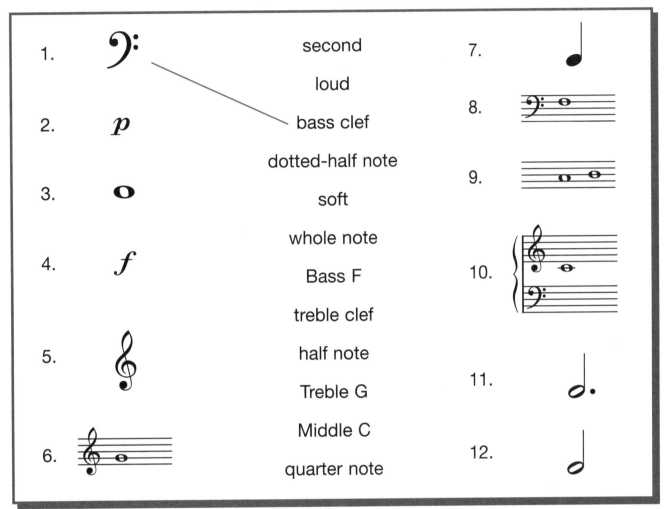

You can check your work!

B A S S C L E F

If you have found the right name for each sign, the words will fit into this crossword puzzle.

21

The Interval of a 5th

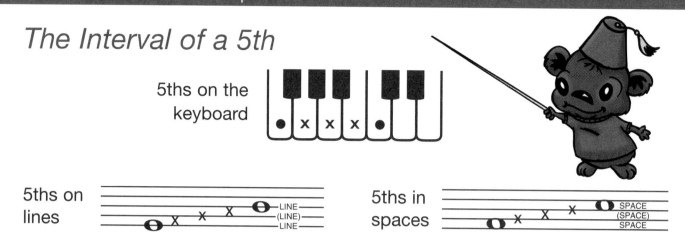

5ths on the keyboard

5ths on lines

5ths in spaces

On the Keyboard

In this jumble, circle all the keyboards that have 5ths.

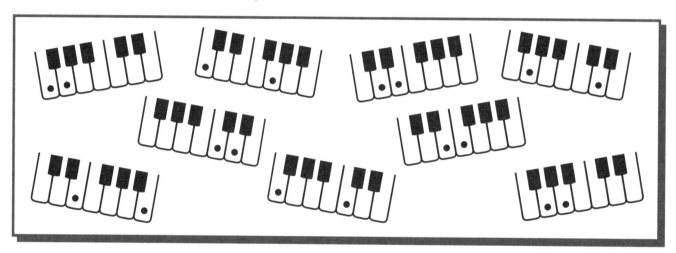

How many 5ths did you find? _____

On the Staff

In this jumble, circle all the 5ths.

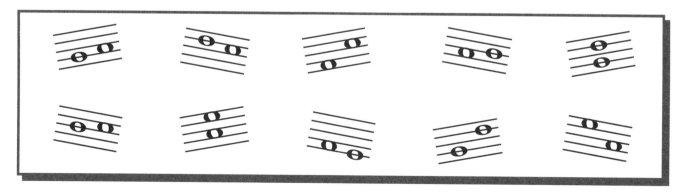

Mark all the 5ths.

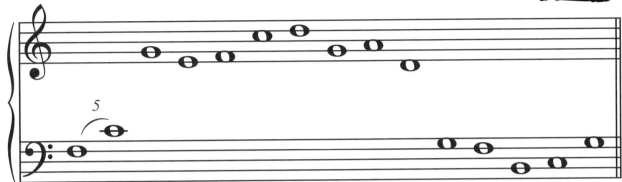

On the keyboard write the letter name of each note.

  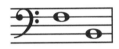

Spot-Placing

To find each note:
- Put an X on the Landmark line.
- Spot-place the note and write its name in the box.
- Then play and name the note.

1.  ☐

2.  ☐

3.   ☐

4.   ☐

23

Rhythm

Complete each incomplete measure with *one* note.

In each of these rhythms, set a strong rhythmic pulse:

1. Point and count — point to each note as you count aloud.

2. Tap and count — tap lightly with your fingertips on the keyboard cover or table — one tap for each **note**.

3. Play and count — LH on a Landmark, RH up a 5th.

Follow the signs for phrasing!

24

Rhythm Detective

Find and circle the measures that have too few pulses.

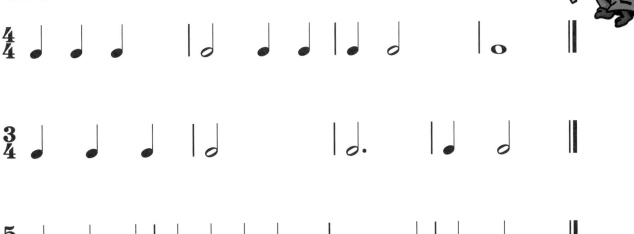

Matching

Match the note value in each box to the notes below:

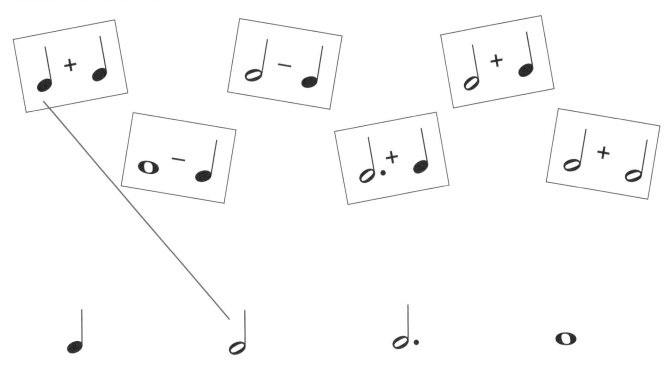

Sight-Playing

1. Circle the clef. Then prepare your hand/s and fingers on the correct keys.

2. Set a **slow** tempo, counting two measures out loud in a strong rhythmic pulse.

3. Play and count with a full tone, **no stopping** from beginning to end.

Except for No. 5, play each piece in the clef in which it is written, then an octave higher or lower with the other hand.

1.

2.

3.

4.

5.

Signs and Terms

Label each tag:

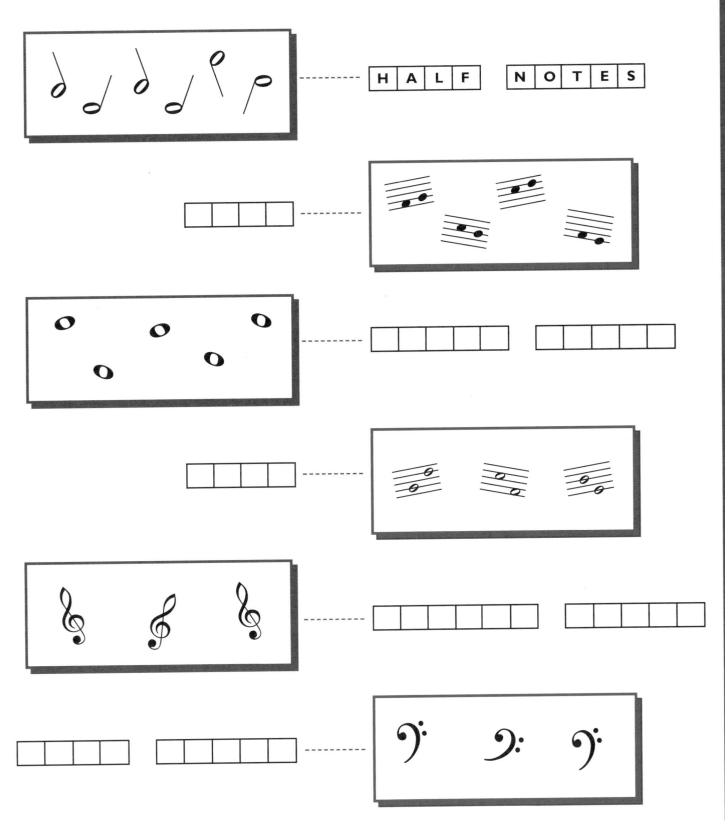

H A L F   N O T E S

27

The Interval of a 3rd

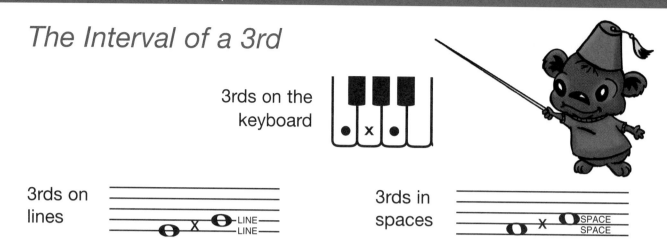

3rds on the
keyboard

3rds on
lines

3rds in
spaces

On the Keyboard

In this jumble, circle all the keyboards that have 3rds.

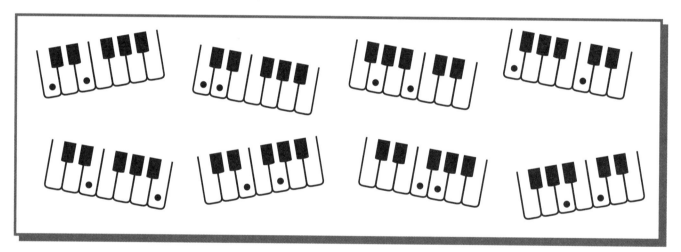

On the Staff

In this jumble, circle all the 3rds.

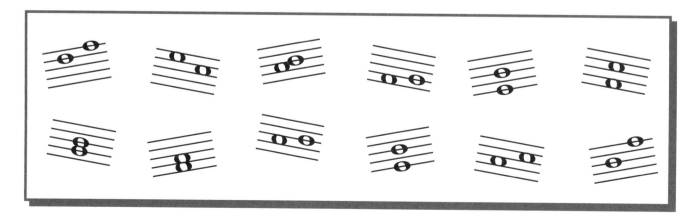

For correlated Discoveries, Repertoire and Technic, see MUSIC TREE 1, pages 27-32.

Keyboard Dictation

Play each group of intervals and write the name of the last note.
Your answers should spell a word.

RH, begin with finger 4:

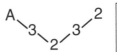 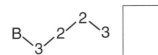 **A**

LH, begin with finger 2:

Spot-Placing

To find each note:
- Put an X on the Landmark line.
- Spot-place the note and write its name in the box.
- Then play and name the note.

1.

2.

3.

4.

5.

6.

Rhythm

In each of these rhythms, set a strong rhythmic pulse:

1. Point and count the rhythm.

2. Walk the rhythm as you count aloud,
   taking one step for each **pulse**.

3. Then walk the rhythm again, taking one step for each **note**.

Watch out! This is new.

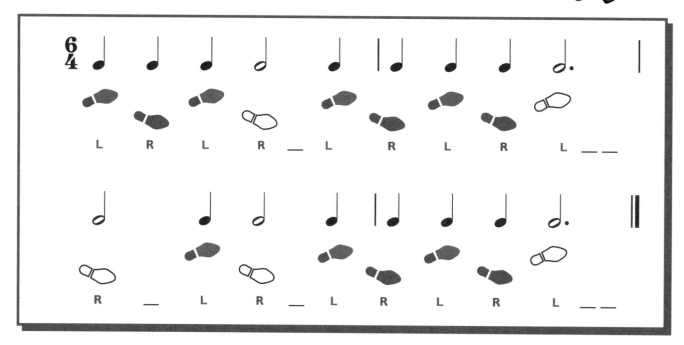

Complete each incomplete measure with **one** note.

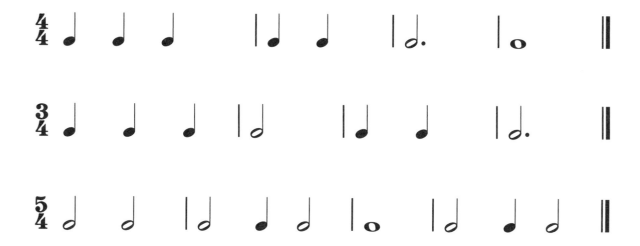

In this rhythm, set a strong rhythmic pulse:

1. Point and count the RH.

2. Tap and count — first, tap the RH;
then, tap hands together.

3. Play and count —
RH on a Landmark, LH down a 3rd.

**Follow the
signs for
_f_ and _p_
as you play!**

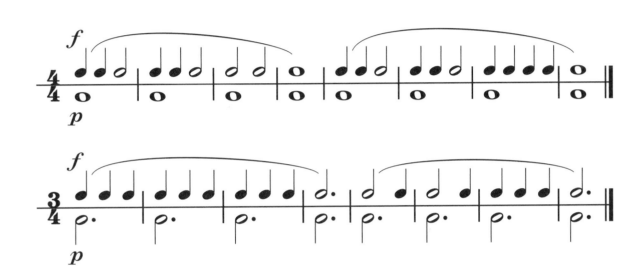

Add the time signature to each of these rhythms.

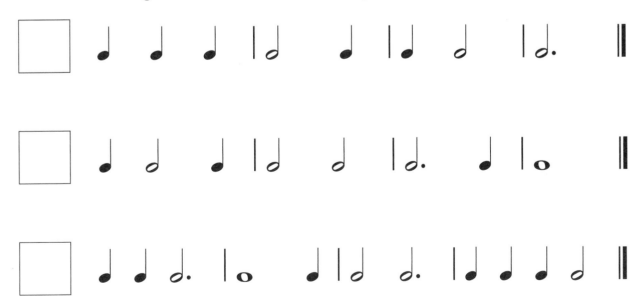

Sight-Playing

There are lots of 5ths in these pieces.

Be sure your five fingers are lying on five neighbor keys —
5ths are always played with fingers 1 and 5!
Eyes on the music — not on your hands!

Except for No. 5, play each piece in the clef in which it is written, then an octave higher or lower with the other hand.

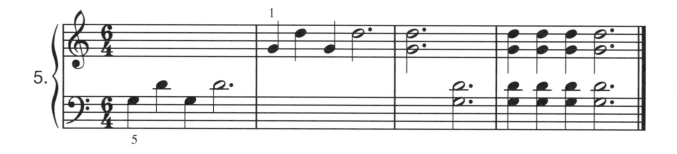

Which One?

Draw lines to connect each note with its letter name.

A

B

C

D

E

F

G

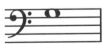

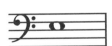
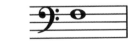

A

B

C

D

E

F

G

33

More about 3rds

Mark all the 3rds.

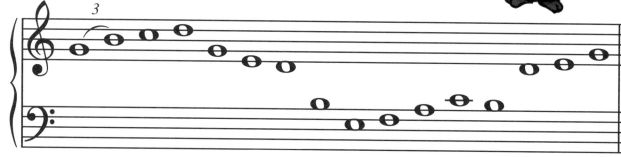

How many line-line 3rds did you find? _____ space-space 3rds? _____

Write and name the note a 3rd **above** each of these notes.

Write and name the note a 3rd **below** each of these notes.

For correlated Discoveries, Repertoire and Technic, see MUSIC TREE 1, pages 33-39.

Keyboard Dictation

Your answers should spell a word!

Play each group of intervals.
Then write the name of the last note.

RH, begin with finger 5:

   ☐   ☐   ☐

LH, begin with finger 5:

☐   ☐   ☐

Spot-Placing

Each of these notes is a 2nd, 3rd, or 5th above or below a Landmark.

To find each note:
- Put an X on the Landmark line.
- Spot-place the note and write its name in the box.
- Then play and name the note.

1. ☐

2. ☐

3.  ☐

4.  ☐

5. 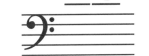 ☐

6. 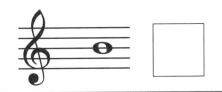 ☐

35

Rhythm

In each of these rhythms, set a strong rhythmic pulse:

1. Point and count — point to each note as you count aloud.

2. Tap and count — tap lightly with your fingertips on the keyboard cover or a table — one tap for each **note**.

3. Play and count — LH on a landmark, RH up a 3rd.

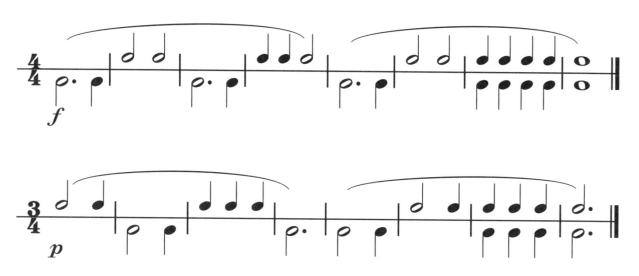

When you tap and count — first, tap the LH; then, tap hands together.

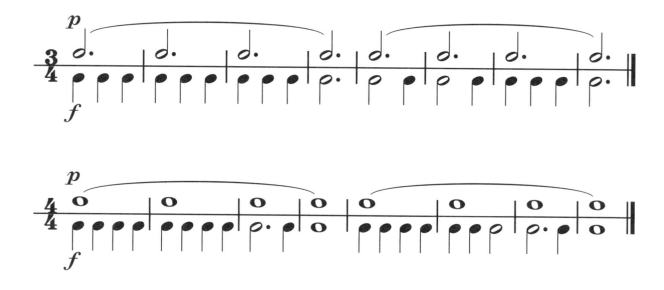

Add the time signature to each of these rhythms.

Complete each incomplete measure with **one** note.

Match the boxes that have the same number of beats.

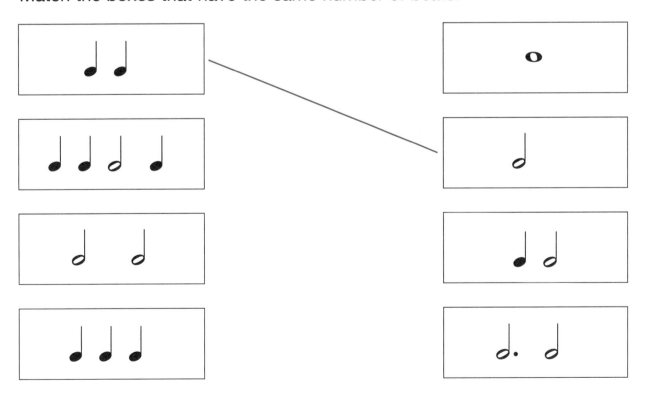

Sight-Playing

Don't forget! A slow tempo and full tone will help you succeed!

Eyes on the music — not on your hands!

1.

2.

3.

4.

5.

Maze

Help Bobo find his way through the maze by following all the thirds.

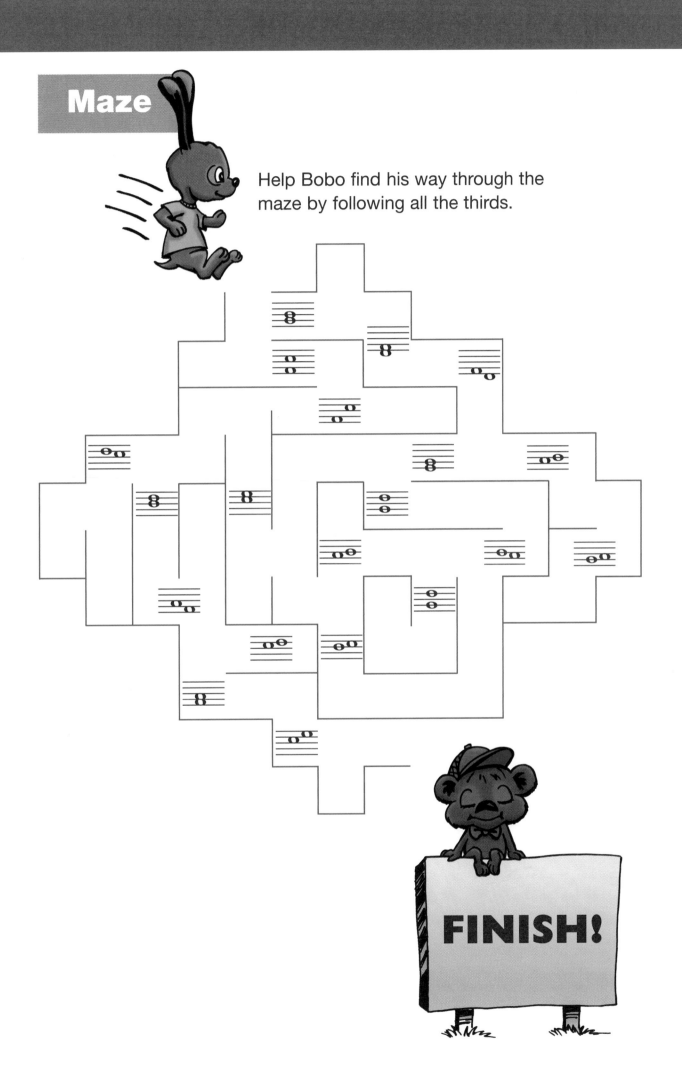

FINISH!

The Interval of a 4th

4ths on the keyboard

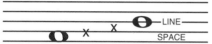

4ths on the staff

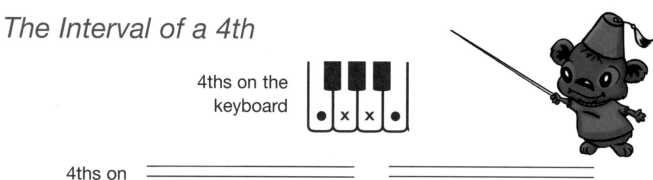

On the Keyboard

In this jumble, circle all the keyboards that have 4ths. How many did you find? _____

On the Staff

In this jumble, circle all the 4ths. How many did you find? _____

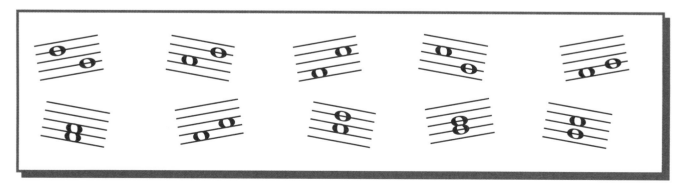

Mark all the 4ths.

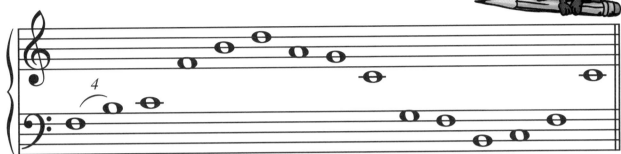

Write the 4th **above** each note.

Write the 4th **below** each note.

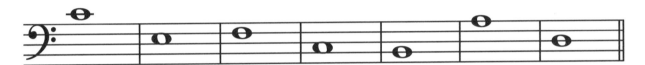

Keyboard Dictation

Play each group of intervals.
Then write the name of the last note.

Your answers should spell a word!

RH, begin with finger 2:

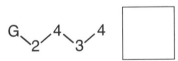

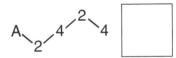

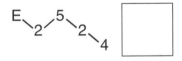

LH, begin with finger 2:

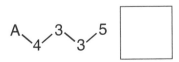

Write and name the 4th **above** each Landmark.

Write and name the 4th **below** each Landmark.

Now play and name each note.

Spot-Placing

To find each note:
- Put an X on the Landmark line.
- Spot-place the note and write its name in the box.
- Then play and name the note.

1.

2.

3.

4.

5.

6.

Rhythm

1. Swing and say the rhyme with a strong rhythmic pulse.

2. Say the rhyme again, drawing lines under the words.

3. Then walk the rhythm as you say the rhyme,
   taking one step for each pulse.

Tied notes form **one sound!**

TIE

Camel Ride

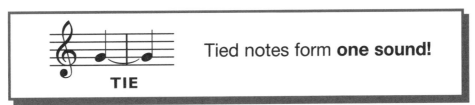

If you can hold ___ on tight, you're in for quite ___ a treat,

If you don't ride ___ him right, you'll end up in ___ the street.

Notes **before** the
first full measure.

UPBEAT

My Horses Ain't Hungry

My hors - es ain't hun - gry; they won't eat your hay.

I'll climb in my sad - dle and ride on my way.

43

In each of these rhythms, set a strong rhythmic pulse:

1. Point and count — point to each note as you count aloud.

2. Tap and count — tap lightly with your fingertips on the
   keyboard cover or a table—one tap for each **note**.

3. Play and count — LH on a Landmark, RH up a 4th.

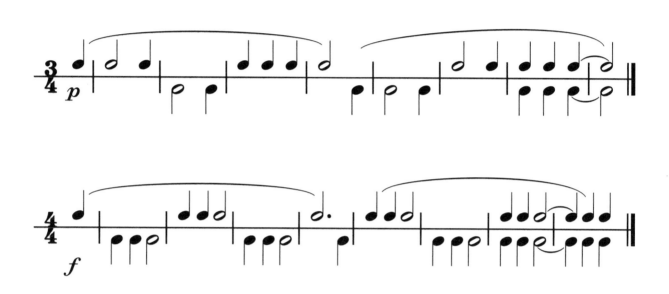

When you tap and count — first, tap the RH; then, tap hands together.

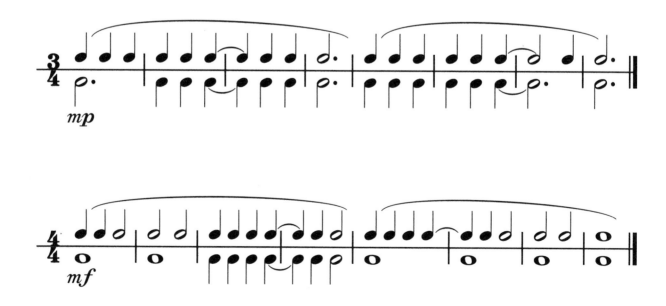

Sight-Playing

Prepare your fingers carefully on the correct keys —
then keep your eyes on the music!

1.

2.

3.

4.

5.

Now play No. 5 again, using fingers $\frac{3}{1}$ throughout.

Noteworthy Puzzle

Write the words spelled by the notes and letters.
The first one is done to show you how.

1.  L | A | B | L | E |

2.  N

3.  R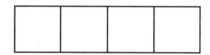

4.

5.  S

6.  T

7. 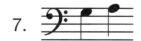 R

Spot-Placing

Each of these notes is a 2nd, 3rd, 4th, or 5th **above** or **below** a Landmark.
  • Put an X on the Landmark line.
  • Spot-place the note and write its name in the blank.

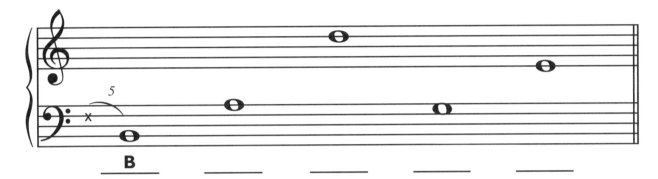

B _____ _____ _____ _____ _____

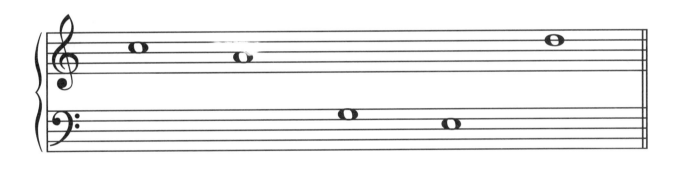

_____ _____ _____ _____ _____

Keyboard Dictation

Play each group of intervals and write the name of the last note.

RH, begin with the thumb.

For correlated Discoveries, Repertoire and Technic, see MUSIC TREE 1, pages 47-51.

Rhythm

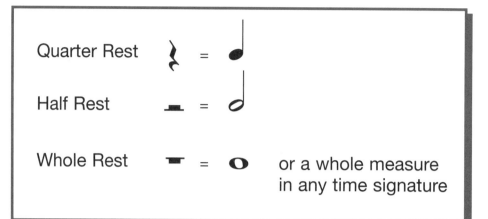

Quarter Rest	𝄽 = ♩	
Half Rest	▬ = 𝅗𝅥	
Whole Rest	▬ = 𝅝	or a whole measure in any time signature

Set a strong rhythmic pulse:

1. Point and count the rhythm.

2. Walk the rhythm as you count aloud, taking one step for each **pulse**.

3. Then walk the rhythm again, taking one step for each **note** or **rest**.

Whisper the rests!

In each of these rhythms, set a strong rhythmic pulse:

1. Point and count — whisper the rests!

2. Tap and count.

3. Play and count — RH on a Landmark, LH down a 4th.

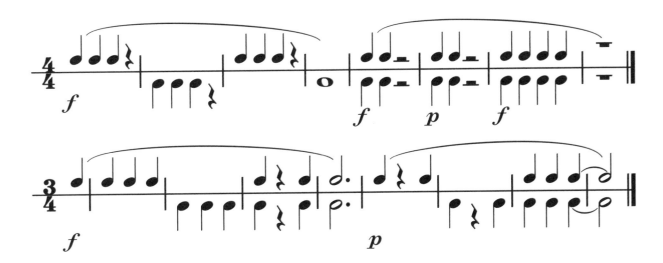

Trace these rests:

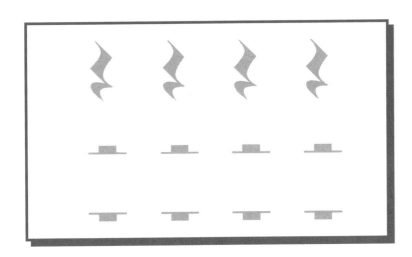

Draw 4 quarter rests: Draw two half rests: Draw one whole rest:

Sight-Playing

Look at all those 4ths!
Eyes on the music, not on your hands!

1.

2.

3.

4.

5.

Now play No. 5 again, using fingers $\frac{5}{2}$ throughout.

Rhythm Puzzle

At the bottom of the page are five lines on which to write five short sentences.
The note(s) and/or rest(s) in each box are clues to which words to use.
For example, to complete sentence 1, use words from boxes with one pulse;
to complete sentence 2, use words from boxes with two pulses, etc.
Your answers should create a set of Sight-Playing steps!

♩	𝅝 + 𝄽	♩ + ♩	♩ + ♩	♩	♩. + 𝄽
Set	No	Play	Count	Prepare	and
♩.	♩ + ♩.	𝄽	▬	♩ – 𝄽	♩ + ▬
two	stopping	hands	a	and	count
▬ + ♩.	♩. + ♩	♩ + 𝄽	𝅝 + ♩	𝅝	𝅝 – 𝄽
from	with	slow	beginning	a	measures.
▬ – ♩	♩ + 𝄽 + ♩	♩ + ♩	▬ + ♩	𝅝 + ♩	♩ + ♩ + ♩
fingers.	to	tempo.	full	end.	tone.

1. _____

2. _____

3. _____

4. _____

5. _____

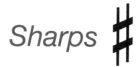

Sharps

A sharp sign (♯) in front of a note means to play that note on the very next key HIGHER.

With RH fingers 2-3 play C-C♯, D-D♯, E-E♯, etc. up to C.

Most sharps are played on **black** keys.
Which two sharps are played on **white** keys? _____ and _____

On the keyboard below, put an X on the keys you will play.

Then, on the staff, circle the two sharps played on **white** keys.

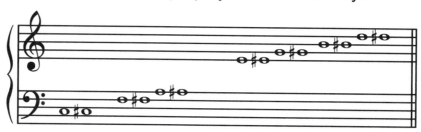

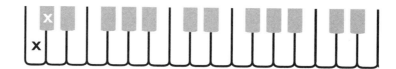

Play and name each key you checked.

Trace these sharp signs: Be sure the line or space shows in the "window" of the sharp.

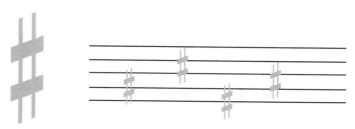

For correlated Discoveries, Repertoire and Technic, see MUSIC TREE 1, pages 52-57.

Flats ♭

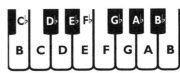

A flat sign (♭) in front of a note means to play that note on the very next key LOWER.

With LH fingers 2-3 play C-C♭, B-B♭, A-A♭, etc. down to C.

Most flats are played on **black** keys.
Which two flats are played on **white** keys? _____ and _____

On the keyboard below, put an X on the keys you will play.

Then, on the staff, circle the two flats played on **white** keys.

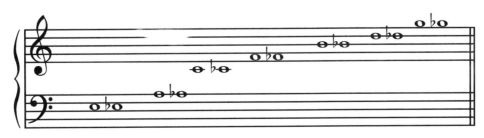

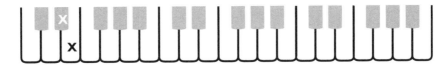

Play and name each key you checked.

Trace these flat signs: Be sure the line or space shows in the "window" of the flat.

Rhythm

In each of these rhythms, set a strong rhythmic pulse:

1. Point and count (whisper the rests!).

2. Tap and count.

3. Play and count — LH on F♯, RH on C♯.

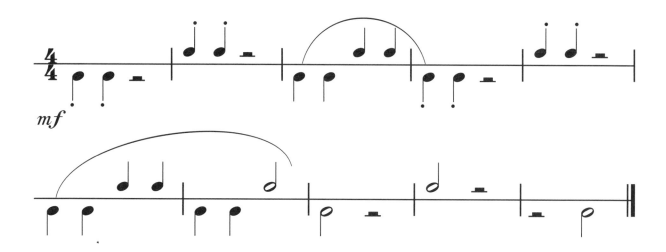

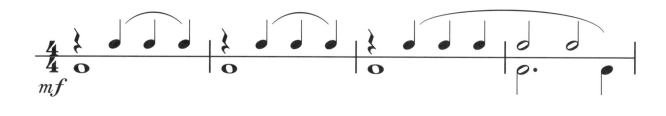

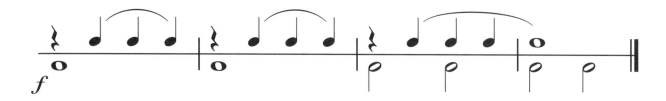

Music Math

Complete each incomplete measure with one **rest**.

Add or subtract the notes or rests in each problem.
Use **notes** to write your answer.

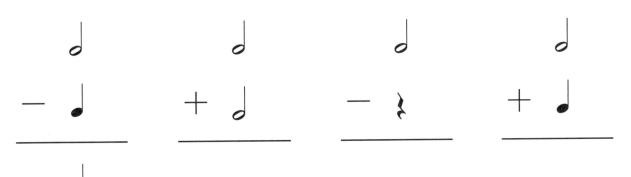

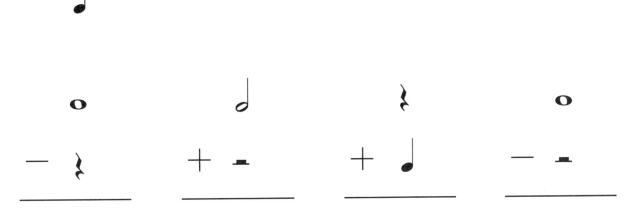

Sight-Playing

Keep a steady tempo —slow enough so that you play accurately on the first reading. Count as you play, and whisper the rests!

1.

2.

3.

4.

5.

Now combine Nos. 4 and 5 and play them hands together!

Crossword Puzzle

ACROSS

2.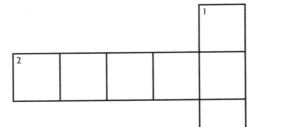

3. ♭

4. ⌢

6.

7.

9.

10.

DOWN

1. ▬

4.

5. 𝄾

8. 𝄿

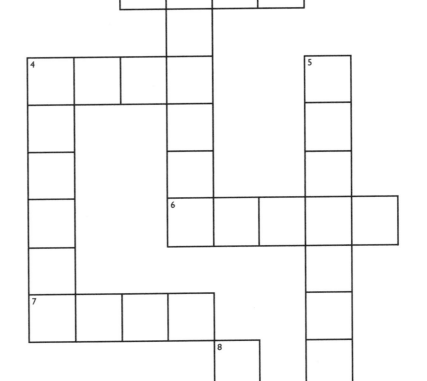

Sharps (♯) last through a Measure

A sharp in front of a note sharps all the notes on the same line or space throughout that measure. The next barline after a sharp cancels it.

Circle all the notes you will sharp. How many did you find? _____

Flats (♭) last through a Measure

A flat in front of a note flats all the notes on the same line or space throughout that measure. The next barline after a flat cancels it.

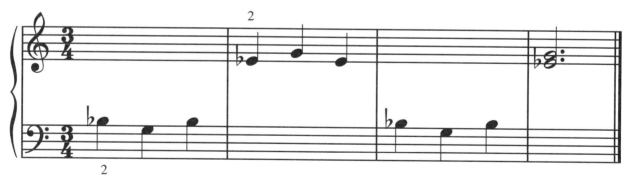

Circle all the notes you will flat. How many did you find? _____

Naturals

A natural sign (♮) cancels a sharp or flat within a measure. It means to play the note on its natural key.

On the keyboard under the staff, put an X on the keys you will play.
Then play and name each pair of keys.

Naturals are **always** played on white keys.

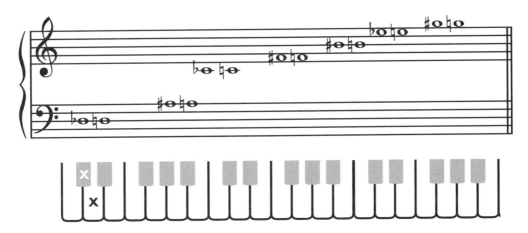

Trace these natural signs:

Be sure the line or space shows in the "window" of the natural.

Trace the sharp, flat and natural signs on this staff.
Then play and name the notes in each measure.

Rhythm

In each of these rhythms, set a strong rhythmic pulse:

1. Point and count — point to each note as you count aloud.

2. Tap and count — tap lightly with your fingertips on the keyboard cover or a table — one tap for each **note**.

3. Play and count — RH on A♭, LH on E♭.

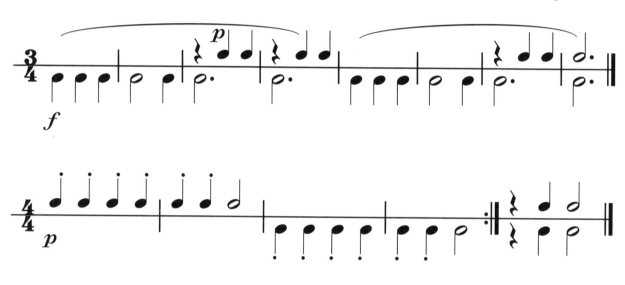

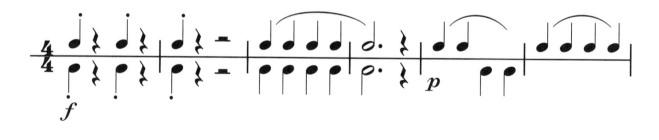

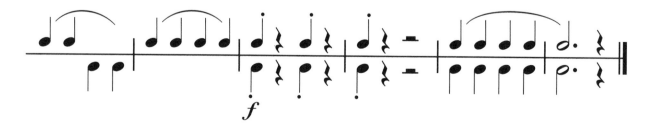

Rhythm Detective

Add the time signature to each of these rhythms.

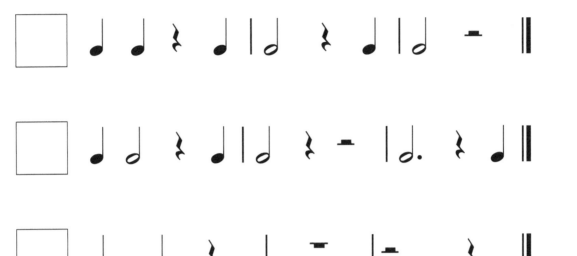

Matching

Match the boxes that have the same number of pulses.

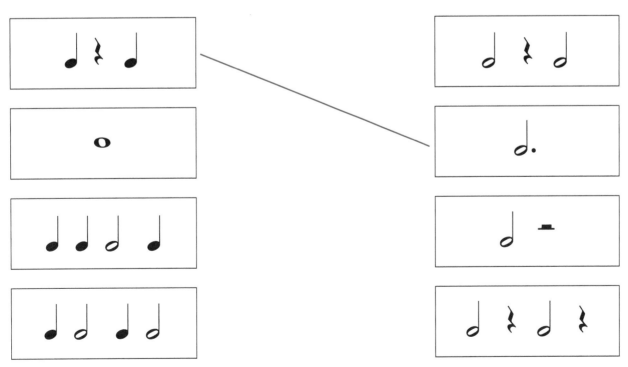

Sight-Playing

When you prepare your fingers on the keys,
be sure to prepare for sharps or flats, too.

Now combine Nos. 4 and 5 play them hands together!

Matching

Draw a line to connect each sign with its name.

medium soft

natural

quarter rest

sharp

flat

5th in spaces

upbeat

3rd on lines

repeat sign

4th

mf

tie

half rest

slur

staccato notes

medium loud

whole rest

5th on lines

3rd in spaces

mp

Glossary

	8va - - - - - ⌐	Play notes one octave higher
	8va - - - - - ⌐	Play notes one octave lower
2nd		From one line to the very next space, or one space to the very next line.
3rd		From one line to the next line, or one space to the next space.
4th		From line to space, skipping one line; or space to line, skipping one space.
5th		From space to space, skipping a space; or line to line, skipping a line.
	p	*piano,* Italian for soft
	mp	*mezzo piano,* Italian for medium soft
	mf	*mezzo forte,* Italian for medium loud
	f	*forte,* Italian for loud
quarter rest	𝄽	silence as long as a quarter note
half rest	▬	silence as long as two quarter notes
whole rest	▬	a whole measure of silence in any time signature
flat	♭	play the very next key lower
sharp	♯	play the very next key higher
natural	♮	cancels a sharp or flat within a measure
repeat sign	:‖	play the piece a second time
staccato	♪̇	short or detached
tie	⌢	A curved line connecting two successive notes of the same pitch. Tied notes form one sound as long as the value of the two notes together.
upbeat	♩ ♩ ♩ ♩	Notes that come before the first full measure of a piece.